10 TIPS
FOR
HOMEBUYERS

HOW NOT TO SCREW UP YOUR PURCHASE AND SUCCESSFULLY GET TO THE CLOSING TABLE

ESSENTIAL INFORMATION YOU NEED TO KNOW

Carol Pro Murray

This book is dedicated to all the Realtors® who give 100% to their buyer clients, those who work tirelessly for months to find that "home", and those that find that "home" in one afternoon out. This book is also dedicated to the many mortgage representatives, brokers, lenders, and bankers who commit themselves to working with their clients, and overcoming financial trials to get them to the closing table. Some come easier than others.

Table of Contents

Foreword

The ideas and insights in this book are gathered from my own experience of actively selling real estate. This is not a complete list of how not to screw up your home purchase, that would be impossible to guarantee. We all go into "the process" with the best intentions. For the most part, with guidance from professionals, you'll be just fine.

Acknowledgment

Thank you to my many clients and cooperating agents throughout the years. Every transaction has taught me something different. You have all added to my bank of knowledge. Thank you also to my brokerage, Keller Williams Lakeside, its management, and all of the mentors who continue to impart their knowledge for us to continually grow and become better agents. And I would be remiss if I didn't acknowledge the great associates of NCI, School of Real Estate for their classes and continuing education every year.

CHAPTER 1
You're Not Your Brother-in-Law

Ah, house hunting. There's nothing quite like the thrill of finding your dream home and taking that leap into home ownership. But with all the big decisions to make, it can be overwhelming and no one likes to make a mistake, especially when it comes to making such a big purchase as buying your home. But more often than not, homeowners find themselves overlooking important details and missing out on key things that could have made their purchase go much smoother.

But fear not: here are a few tips on how NOT to screw up your home-buying purchase.

First and foremost, while it can be tempting to rely on advice from well-meaning family members and friends, this is not the best source for advice. Sure, they may have had positive experiences with their home purchases. But remember: everyone's situation is different. What worked for your brother-in-law may not work for you. Every buyer has different needs and since the real estate market is continually changing, you'll need to find what works for you.

Have realistic expectations: Finances can be tricky but it's important to be mindful of them when buying a house; this is not an investment that will double in value overnight! Although, owning real estate is one of the best ways to increase your wealth.

Make a wish list: What do you want in your dream home? Write it all down! Of course, you won't get everything on your list but having a clear idea of what you're looking for will help narrow down the search. Be willing to make concessions. Maybe you won't get the updated bathroom you wanted, however, the home backs up to a nature preserve. What's more important to you at this particular time?

It's best to seek out an unbiased professional whose expertise will help you make informed decisions. Of course, I'm going to suggest using a Realtor® and finding a Mortgage Loan Representative to work with.

CHAPTER 2
That Scary Word, Credit

Get organized: We know – paperwork is a bore! But it's important to get all your documents together before starting the process; having everything ready ahead of time will save you time and stress in the long run.

DON'T assume that your credit is good enough for a home purchase. Experian, TransUnion, and Equifax all provide free access to your credit report at www.annualcreditreport.com—use this resource to check your credit score before you apply for a mortgage loan. It could save you from making an expensive mistake down the road! And, if you don't have a credit score in the first place, then it can be nearly impossible to get approved for a loan, without having to open a credit card and provide a history of creditworthiness.

Set a budget: It's easy to get carried away… so set aside some time to figure out exactly how much you can afford each month for mortgage payments, taxes, and other related costs. Knowing this information ahead of time will be extremely useful as you start looking around.

DON'T go making large purchases on credit right BEFORE you apply for a mortgage. This can drastically lower your credit score. A mortgage loan officer worth their weight in gold will inform you once they pre-approve you with the same advice. Not only will your credit score lower, but your debt will also increase, thus making qualifying for a mortgage that much more difficult. Do your research and make sure you understand what kind of mortgage product is best for you. There are all different products and many of them include low down payments, and/or no closing costs, first-time buyer grants, and more. A word of warning though, don't keep "applying" at different banks or with different mortgage representatives, your credit report will show all of the inquiries. Not good. Don't worry about the interest rate you're getting today. It may change before you find your house. Now that you've buttoned up the mortgage part, and are ready to go with your pre-approval in hand (not literally, as it's probably a pdf you saved on your desktop), and you're aware of what you can afford, now it's time to get serious. You may by this point have begun working with a Realtor® who told you to get pre-approved first, but now you can safely go and view homes without the worry of missing out. Most sellers are weary to accept an offer that isn't accompanied by a vetted buyer. In addition, you don't want to fall in love with a home and have your agent write an offer. They more than likely will, however again, the chances are low that your offer will be taken seriously.

CHAPTER 3
We Love Your Parents, However

Get informed: Research the neighborhoods and local real estate markets thoroughly. What's the area like? Are there any planned developments or construction projects in your target neighborhood? You want to be sure that you're making an informed decision! If you have school-aged children, where are the schools located? Or, if you'd rather not be near a school, you'll need to know that too.

Who's buying the house? You or your parents?

So, you may not want to bring your parents along until you have found a home you love and have written an offer on it. Who knows, they may wind up being more of a hindrance than a help in this situation. Most parents, although their heart is in the right place, tend to notice EVERYTHING wrong with a house. This isn't necessarily bad, although if you're touring multiple homes in an appointment then it will take forever to get through them all. Plus, even when the parent knows the house isn't going to be "the one", they'll still insist on making their home-owning knowledge heard and will usually throw in "that's gonna cost ya" just for fun.

I'm all for having your folks or other well-meaning individuals see the home you're purchasing, I'm just suggesting, for the Realtor®s sanity (not imperative), bring them in during the inspection. discussed more in Chapter 8.

CHAPTER 4
Proceed on Autopilot

Once the inspection is complete and your loan is in process, DON'T do anything but breathe and go to work! Don't be tempted to add any more debt or try anything else that could change your credit score while it's being processed. Don't go looking for that new couch or dining room table, even if the salesperson tells you that you don't have to make payments for three years, it will still show up on your credit report. Feel free to browse the internet, but stay out of the stores if you're weak.

DON'T quit your job for another job. Yes, you heard me correctly. DO NOT change jobs (if you must) wait until after the closing has occurred and you are officially a homeowner. Of course, why would you want to quit now, you have a mortgage to pay! I've experienced a buyer, not my buyer, as I was the listing agent representing the seller, who quit her job on a Friday. The closing was scheduled for the following Monday. Wouldn't you know it, the underwriter of the loan (bank/mortgage company) went to re-verify the employment of the buyer on that Friday. The human resource representative said she no longer worked there, she just quit. Well, guess what, she didn't get that home and my seller was less than thrilled that the home sale fell through. In the buyer's head, she figured the new job, which was starting on Monday, was for more money so what was the problem? The problem was she no longer proved stable employment, which was what she had at the onset of the application. Plus, if the role is in a different capacity or you've decided to become self-employed or an entrepreneur then all bets are really off the table. That was a tough pill to swallow, for all parties involved!

CHAPTER 5
Guard Your
Financial Well-Being

Do understand more info may be required and you may be asked to provide documents or more information during the underwriting process. It's best to remain calm throughout – just make sure you stay ahead of any deadlines that are set by your lender. If you're using funds from retirement accounts or other accounts don't just pull the money out. Your lender will want to prove the money is yours and that you have reserves for additional payments. Keep in mind that the underwriter at your mortgage company or bank may conditionally approve you, so make sure to address any conditions and get them cleared to move forward.

Sometimes it can feel that the underwriting process is taking forever. Keep in mind the underwriter's job is to ultimately approve or deny your loan. Of course, we'd always prefer a quick answer, although in reality there are several documents to be reviewed and vetting that needs to be completed first. Many lenders now use a desktop underwriting system, which can "conditionally" approve you even before you have secured a property.

Just don't forget one very important thing: no matter what, don't co-sign for someone else during this process. Your future and finances are too important to risk! As hard as this one may be, especially if you've been put in the position, DON'T do it! This will put your credit at risk, and the debt will show up on your credit report, thus your debts will increase, and you may not qualify now for a mortgage.

CHAPTER 6
Hire A Professional

What SHOULD you do when attempting to purchase a house?

Hire a professional real estate agent or broker, as a Buyer's Agent. They can help you explain the entire buying process and will obligate themselves to go to bat for you in negotiation, their fiduciary duty will be to you. By having an Exclusive Buyer Agency Agreement in place they are working for you and will ensure your best interests are being considered at all times. In the long run, this could save you thousands of dollars. If you call the number on the sign, that agent is representing the seller. Of course, they may want to make more money by being the only agent involved, but can you be sure you're getting the real deal? Their fiduciary duty is to the seller.

Why would someone want to be represented by someone else who doesn't have their best interest? And really, at the end of the day aren't we, the Realtor®, there to uphold our code of ethics? I know, you're thinking the seller will pay less, so I can get it for less. Not always true. Plus, the agent isn't getting paid directly, the brokerage gets paid who then pays the agent. Just saying, it would benefit you to use an ABR®, which would be an Accredited Buyer's Representative. They will disclose what they know about the seller to you, they will keep your information confidential, and you'll have better results because they are expert negotiators, as they have to have several successful buyer-side closings to become designated. You will receive a higher level of service, something I believe every buyer would want. You can find an ABR® designee on the National Association of Realtors® website. www.nar.realtor.

CHAPTER 7
This Isn't The Limbo Dance

You found the house, now what? Don't lowball your offer! You're not in a limbo line. This is a waste of time and it's not professional. Make sure you make a market sensible decision if you like the house. Many sellers will immediately become aggravated and will want to just reject your offer. If you're lucky, the listing agent will be able to convince the seller to counter. Although, I've witnessed lowball offers getting thrown out immediately, and what could have led to a successful sale winds up never happening. You don't need to bid thousands of dollars over asking either. For a bit of reference, $1000 over the asking price can equate to less than $15 a month in some situations. This is when it's good to call your lender and make sure you're equipped with the knowledge of how much you can afford monthly, including taxes, homeowner's insurance, and possibly mortgage insurance.

Ask the lender how much it would be if you went $5000 over, or even if you offered to pay some of the seller's closing costs, would you still have enough to close? If you don't want to bid at asking or overbid, then possibly offer the seller free occupancy for a certain number of days. Typically, once you close on your home your mortgage payment won't begin until 30 days after the closing date, and at the beginning of the month. Say you close on Friday, Feb. 10, 2023, your first payment would be due on April 1, 2023. That gives you time before you make your payment, and the seller doesn't have to pay you or someone else rent during those 30 days. You're not making a double payment if you're currently renting. They're out of the house on March 12th and you still have a couple of weeks before your first mortgage payment is due.

Of course, I don't suggest you always do this when you make an offer. Situations are different and it depends on the competition there is. But be very careful, this strategy only works if you're confident they'll leave the house in good condition. Currently, at least in Michigan, we cannot hold a security deposit for damages on a purchase. This gets into leasing, and landlord/tenant laws. Of course, every brokerage is different, so be sure to check with your agent to see what the broker allows.

CHAPTER 8
Don't Skip This Step

Once you have submitted your offer, it's time for the inspection. That's when the professional inspector is there and will do what they're paid to do. They will note any major issues with the home, such as roofing, plumbing, foundation, and electrical issues. They carry a great wealth of information and will give their honest opinion without terrifying you. Also, you may be wanting to bring in Uncle Herb and save the money on a professional inspection, as he's done all the handy work for all the family for the past 40 years, but is he a certified and insured inspector? Will he go up into the attic or climb on top of the roof? Be sure to do your due diligence and research qualified inspectors. Your agent will likely have a list of preferred vendors they will give you.

Make sure you SHOW UP at the inspection! It is wise to follow the inspector around and ask questions. This could save you from having to make major repairs in the near future, as well as give you knowledge on how things work and what you should do periodically. I mentioned the inspection phase earlier in this book. It's an important one. I never advocate for someone to NOT include an inspection clause in their offer. In the event you find a major repair at inspection, you can negotiate for the seller to make that repair. This is also at their discretion. Additionally, this may be a good time to ask the sellers to provide a one-year home warranty for you.

Some inspections lead to the discovery of safety issues in the home. Anything to do with electrical should be appropriately handled. Also, minuscule gas leaks from piping should definitely be addressed. Depending on the type of loan you're acquiring, some lenders may insist on safety issues being fixed.

CHAPTER 9

Lender's Turn

What happens next is the appraisal. The appraisal is ordered by the lender and it is done so to determine the fair market value of the home. They will want to determine that the home is worth at least as much as the loan amount. The value of the home could be at or above market value if there has been an escalation in prices within the last 30 days, due to the competition of buyers. Most appraisers look at comps within the last 90 to 180 days, so if the market has changed in those 3 to 6 months it may affect the sale. Likewise, values may have fallen, and your purchase price may not be supported now. Again, there may be a negotiating period if the home comes in less than value, or if the buyers aren't putting down an adequate amount of money to cover the difference. Most purchase agreements have a clause in them that address this.

If you end up in a position where the home appraised for less than the purchase price, try to work with your agent on negotiating a win-win for both you and the seller. Sometimes it is a financial issue and you don't have extra funds to bring to closing. Sometimes a lender will seek a reconsideration of value, or you may want to order a second appraisal. Granted, no one wants to pay more for a home than it's worth, but keep in mind this is one person's opinion. You've come this far and invested money in the process, don't throw the baby out with the bath water. Once the appraisal is in and negotiated if needed, then your file will go into underwriting for approval or conditional approval.

CHAPTER 10
One Last Look, Sign on The Line

Once you have the clear, your agent will work with the co-op agent and the title companies to set up your closing. It's important to remember that you should always do a walk-through before closing, even if you're giving the seller occupancy. I cannot stress how important this is! What if the seller didn't remove their items? What if they broke something after inspection and before closing? Even though you may have had an inspection, your agent can help check on any repairs that were negotiated and make sure everything is complete for the close of escrow. Every step in the process is important, but this one has been known to save buyers thousands of dollars. You know you're getting what you bargained for when it's time to sign on the dotted line.

Your lender will provide you with the numbers (a dollar amount) you need for closing. Usually, money is either wired to the title company or a certified check made out to the title company is accepted. Please do not bring cash. There is nothing worse than a buyer walking in with a knapsack filled with cash. And yes, it has happened.

Your agent will remind you to have the utilities put into your name. This is very important. If you don't have them transferred into your name, they may end up being shut off. That's the last thing anyone wants. Utility companies have the ability to shut off your service remotely. And if it does get shut off, they'll charge you, the new buyer to turn it back on, which may take days. Interestingly enough, I always found it odd utility companies can shut off remotely, but will not turn them back on remotely. There's a fee for everything, thus is the way of the world.

You've done it! You made it to the closing table and successfully purchased your home! You didn't screw up! Congratulations on being a homeowner!

Conclusion

Remember if at any point you get stuck or confused, there are plenty of professionals out there who can help you understand what's going on in the process of buying a home. Don't be afraid to ask questions. The more you know, the easier it will be to purchase that perfect house for you and your family. Good luck!

Happy home buying! :)

This concludes my tips and fun antidotes. I hope this has been helpful and I wish you the best of luck in finding that dream home of yours. Take care and happy hunting!

Afterword

I strongly suggest a future or repeat home-buyer work with a Real Estate Professional when looking to purchase a home. If you'd like any additional information, or would like a referral for a vetted, buyer's agent in your area, please don't hesitate to reach out to myself or my colleague, Charles Provenzano, at Keller Williams Lakeside Market Center, Shelby Township, Michigan.

https://carolpro.kw.com/

carolpro@kwlakeside.com

586-685-1250

.